On the Other Side of Through There is HOPE!

McDougal & Associates

Servants of Christ and Stewards of the
Mysteries of God

Eric Roy, Jr.
October 8, 1984 — December 21, 2010

On the Other Side of Through There is HOPE!

By

Dawn Greay

Published by:
McDougal & Associates
18896 Greenwell Springs Road
Greenwell Springs, LA 70739
www.ThePublishedWord.com

McDougal & Associates is dedicated to the spreading of the Gospel of Jesus
Christ to as many people as possible in the shortest time possible.

ISBN 978-1-940461-93-9

Printed on demand in the US, the UK and Australia
For Worldwide Distribution

Dedication

I dedicate this book **to the memory of my son Eric**: It was through his death the birthing of this book came. I pray that mothers who may experience or have previously experienced the loss of a child will be uplifted by it.

I pray that as you read this book, you will find comfort, relief, deliverance and truth. May God make you whole and restored, as He has done and continues to do for me.

I also pray that anyone who has experienced any type of loss—a loved one, a job, a spouse through death or divorce, a car, a house, or any other valuable thing due to a major storm like Hurricanes Katrina and Sandy—may reach out to the Lord of Comfort and allow Him to bring restoration and wholeness to your life.

To my family—Malcolm Sr., Malcolm Jr., Danisha, Barbara and Solomon Jr.: Thank you for your patience, love, prayers and support shown while I went through my experience with God.
Despite the uncertainties of "The Other Side of Through," with God's help, WE CAN MAKE IT! I love all of you and appreciate all that you do to continue to help me move forward on a daily basis.

To my extended family—LaTescia, Lisa, Wanda, Yvette, Oreathe, Valencia, and Rona; Momma Georgetta and Mrs. Frank: I just want you all to know you are dear to my heart and I love you just for being there.

To my Fulfilling the Gospel Ministries International family: Thanks to everyone who labored in prayer on behalf of my family, who came by to speak words of wisdom, and to everyone who served my family in whatever capacity.

Finally, I would love to say thanks to Justin and Marie Hillard of Wrapped in Memories (Flint, Michigan) for allowing God to use your gifts to make the lovely pillow and shawl.

May all of you who have poured into our lives be blessed.

Trust ye in the Lord *for ever: for in the* Lord *Jehovah is everlasting strength.*

Isaiah 26:4 KJV

Contents

Foreword by Apostle Reggie Wilson

I met Dawn Greay while performing at the wedding of a mutual friend, and I immediately recognized that her serious demeanor spoke volumes regarding her attitude. Whatever Dawn puts her hand to, she does with informed commitment, moving beyond mere perfection and aiming for excellence.

Years later, music allowed our paths to intersect once again. It is amazing how commitment to community outreach transforms the hearts and lives, not only of those being served, but also those called upon to serve. Shortly after singing with a praise and worship group, which grew to become a community choir, Dawn and many of her fellow choir members transitioned to being discipled in the Christian faith by my wife Vera and myself at Fulfilling the Gospel Ministries. Through fellowship and relationship building, Dawn and her husband, Malcolm Sr., then became youth pastors in the ministry.

That was many years ago. Then, let's fast-forward a bit. Over time, Dawn became an elder in our ministry and serving in the Kingdom, as an elder in the ministry, requires a total commitment despite oneself and one's circumstances. Dawn was faithful to minister in whatever capacity she was needed. But, be not deceived! Such dedication does have its challenges, obstacles and hurdles. Dawn experienced this with the sudden, unexpected and tragic death of her twenty-six-year-old son, Eric.

The spiritual dynamics of serving God, for Dawn, including her responsibilities, now changed dramatically. There can be no doubt that it came with a cost she never anticipated or even imagined. Yet, through this terrible ordeal, the first of many books has been birthed from her heart to bless others.

Dawn Greay is an amazing writer on the rise, one who has discovered strength from the agonizing experience of pain and grief from unexpected loss. The tragic death of her eldest son, whom she referred to as "my baby," has now propelled her into another dimension of helping others.

Know that if you are ever in the same room with Dawn, your first impression will be a lasting one. Her presence commands attention, and her intelligence demands respect. I am careful to note that since Dawn has undergone this grieving process, I have seen a new heart awakened in her with a higher level of understanding. The compassion of the Father in her and through her now brings hope through to the other side.

This book will, most likely, stir up mixed emotions in the reader, but in the end, I believe you will encounter God. Enjoy your reading, and I will see you on the other side!

Apostle Dr. Reginald H. Wilson Sr.

Introduction

This was the hardest writing project I ever undertook. Many days and nights were spent journaling the painful thoughts and emotions experienced during and after the transition of my son Eric from life to death. It was all something I just could not have prepared myself for.

After Eric's death, I was given book after book that was supposed to bring healing and comfort to a broken heart, and yet there was still an emptiness in me that needed to be filled. It was with that hole in my heart still in place that I sat down and begin to pen my way to healing.

This form of therapy was the beginning of a healing process and a helpful way to release the pain I felt from losing my son. It worked. Writing down the events of what I had come to call "the beginning of my heart's demise" and how I had, with God's help, dealt with the aftermath and all the things in between, I started to see a light of hope.

My writing went through many versions, as I remembered more and more of my thoughts and feelings and sought God about what should be told and what need not be told to help others get though their own grieving process. What you see before you is the final result.

Now, having received healing myself, it is my desire to encourage all those who have experienced some form of loss that brought devastation to their life. Often, when we encounter any type of devastation, we believe we can't or we won't

Introduction

make it. I want you to know that you can, you will and you must make it. Others will benefit from your success and your story. Why not share it as your own form of therapy, as I have done here, and, while you do, watch for the light to appear at the end of the tunnel. The light of hope is what I call it.

Dawn Greay
Marrero, Louisiana

Chapter 1

What a Wild Ride!

Nothing or no one could have ever prepared me for that day nor the events pertaining to it. The hurt and agony of the possibility of losing my baby (although he was already grown) brought me to a terribly confusing state of mind.

Let me take you back through the events as they unfolded and the many thoughts and emotions I experienced and show you how having a relationship with Father God made all the difference in the world.

What a Wild Ride!

When I got up early that morning and started dressing, I noticed that I had missed two phone calls from Eric's best friend. I had also missed phone calls from both my mother's house phone and her cellphone. Curious, I called her to see why she had called my cell phone and not the house phone. I found it very strange indeed that Eric's friend answered my mother's cell phone.

"Miss D," the boy said, "Eric is in the hospital."

I said, "What?"

"He was stabbed," he replied. "It's bad! The knife went into his head, and he's in surgery now. I couldn't get his phone unlocked, so I came over here to your mom's house to call you."

My heart began to pound, and my breath felt as if it had just been squeezed off. I could not breathe, and I had to put my hands over my mouth and force myself to take some slow, deep breaths.

Deep within me was a great scream will-ing itself to come out, but I realized that I had to keep it smothered within because I didn't want to alarm my younger son Malcolm, then sixteen and a junior in high school. I would have to bring myself to a calm state and then think quickly. I didn't want Malcolm to find out just yet the de-tails of what had happened and be upset all day at school.

I called a neighbor who took turns with me taking her son and mine to school and back home. It was my turn, but I asked if she could possibly get the kids to school that morning. She agreed, and Malcolm and I finished getting dressed as quickly as possible, to prepare for whatever the day held for us.

I told Malcolm that I would be there to pick him up from school in the afternoon but that our neighbor would drop him off that morning. As I did this, my mind raced ahead to the hospital and Eric. I needed to get to my baby's side.

When I was finally able to get on the road, it proved to be the longest drive I had ever taken from Slidell to New Orleans. I thought I knew the road well, but that day it was a nightmare.

Fortunately, I was on leave from my job, so that was not a consideration. I tried to get in touch with my husband, who had left earlier that morning for work, to let him know what had happened and that he needed to get to the hospital as soon as possible, but I wasn't able to reach him just then.

I needed to talk to someone, so I called a dear friend, and she did her best to console me and calm me as I drove. While talking to her, however, I begin to break down. It seemed that anxiety had set in and taken over my mind, body and soul. I had to literally command myself to calm down, to pray and to pull myself together. My friend prayed for me, and that helped.

With tears pouring down my face, I drove mindlessly through the rain, praying that God would keep my son alive, touch his body and bring forth healing. Somehow I could hear the voice of the Lord saying to me:

I am in control!
Don't be moved by what you see or hear!
Trust me!

His Word came to mind:

Trust in the LORD with all your heart
  and lean not on your own under-
  standing;
in all your ways submit to him,
  and he will make your paths straight.
                              Proverbs 3:5-6

What a Wild Ride!

I continued talking to my friend on the phone. I screamed, I cried, I prayed and I questioned why? Eric had been such a good child. How could this have happened to him? Where had he been? Who had he been with? How could this have possibly happened?

I once again began to pray. I asked the Lord to help me make it to the hospital safely. "Please don't let me have an accident or get a ticket," I pleaded. I was driving way too fast, especially since it was raining that morning. God heard that prayer and answered it.

All the while, many thoughts ran through my mind about what had happened and why. I decided that, at that point, I didn't really care how it had happened. I just wanted to make it safely to the hospital and make sure Eric was okay. My baby needed me!

CHAPTER 2

The Hospital Scene

I finally made it to the hospital. "Thank You, Lord, for letting me arrive safely," I prayed.

Finding a place to park was difficult. I remember driving up a one-way street and then turning around in the emergency circle to get turned the right way and find a spot to leave the car.

Eric's friend was waiting for me and told me to go to the second floor of the hospital. There I was pointed in the right direction by a security guard. I learned that Eric had just gotten out of surgery and it would be a little while before they allowed me in to see him. I should go to the waiting room, I was told.

When I opened the door to the waiting room, I noticed that it was packed with people of all ages, and many of them were people I knew. They were all there for Eric. My mother and aunt were there, but there were also many of Eric's young friends. Everyone greeted me with eyes full of tears. All that I could think about in that moment was, "Lord, if there ever was a time I needed You, it is now! Help me!"

Several of the young people gathered around me and begin to tell me what they knew about this tragic occurrence. Eric had been at a birthday party, and a fight had broken out. He was nearby and tried to help break it up. One of the men had a knife, and when he lunged for the person he was fighting, Eric happened to be in the way, and the knife struck him instead. "Ma," the boy said, "he didn't do anything wrong. He was just getting something to drink, and then we heard a loud noise. We started to move out of the way, but the next thing we knew, Eric was falling."

"I couldn't do anything," one young man offered. "I saw what happened, and I showed the police who did it."

"There was a nurse at the party," one said, "and she did what she could to help stop the bleeding, but he was hurt bad!"

Others of his friends offered their version of events, and while they did, many things were swirling through my mind.

When I could, I talked to the Lord again. I asked Him to help me keep my sanity. He spoke to my spirit with His Word:

You will keep in perfect peace
those whose minds are steadfast,
because they trust in you. Isaiah 26:3

The Hospital Scene

I had already decided that I really didn't care to know, at the moment, any more about what had happened or how it had happened. I just needed to get to my baby to make sure he was okay or that he was going to be okay. With my knees barely holding the rest of my body up, I made my way to the Intensive Care Unit to see my injured son.

CHAPTER 3

The Sight of My Precious Son

When I finally saw Eric, my heart sank, and I felt physically ill. I could not speak, and I could not believe what I was seeing. My precious son just lay there, totally helpless and unresponsive.

The doctor who had treated Eric decided that he must be placed in an induced coma for a time in the hope that his brain would not swell more. He gave me very little hope that Eric would recover. "He may not even make it through the first twenty-four hours," I was told. "And, if he does return to consciousness, he will probably never regain his motor skills. That means he may never walk again."

It was all too much and I immediately begin to grieve within myself, but then I sensed that God wanted to help me to remain strong for the sake of others who needed to hear a word from Him. I, at least, knew Him, but not everyone there did.

I know it was God Who kept me during those days. As a mother, it was so hard to see my son lying in that hospital bed. It was not the Eric I knew.

I had become accustomed to seeing the fast-moving, on-the-go, happy-go-lucky person. He was always talking, eating or laughing. Now he just lay there, lifeless, with wires connected to him everywhere.

He had done two years of college, majoring in Electrical Engineering at Idaho

State University, and was transferring to the University of New Orleans to begin his junior year. During the summer he was working for The Home Depot in the city, so he had been staying with my mom there.

Now he just lay there. Despite the fact that so many wires from so many machines were connected to various parts of Eric's body, he did come to and seemed to be aware of each of us as we came and went from his side in the following days. That gave me some hope.

Visiting hours in the ICU were at 10 AM, 1 PM, 5 PM and 8 PM, and I was there every single time. My husband came later that first day, and Malcolm Jr. came many days after school. We would all pray with Eric, read the Bible with him and sing songs of worship. But Eric had been severely wounded, and he did not seem to be improving as first days and then weeks passed.

The Sight of My Precious Son

Even after several weeks had passed, the hospital waiting room was still full of people who had come to see how Eric was doing or to share their stories about him. At one point, the security officer on that floor asked me if I would tell them all to go home. He had spoken to several of them, but they didn't seem to be listening and refused to leave.

The problem was that other families couldn't have visitors because there was no space for them. I told him I would do my best to help clear the room. But, at the same time, I didn't want to talk to everyone or entertain their questions. At that point, I still didn't have any answers for them. I was still searching for my own answers.

From the beginning, many of Eric's friends wanted desperately to see him, and the first few days we allowed some of them, along with family members and coworkers, to visit Him. My mother is also a believer, and she and I felt that it was a great opportunity for us to minister to all of those people. So, every person who came to see Eric heard more or less the same Gospel message.

"Take a good look at Eric!" we told them. "This could be you lying there. I know you want to help him, to pray for him, but to do that you first need to have a personal relationship with the Lord Jesus. Then you can pray on Eric's behalf."

We took full advantage of this opportunity, praying for each person who came to Eric's side. Those who did not have a personal relationship with the Lord were encouraged to pray a prayer of repentance and ask Jesus to come into their hearts and become the Lord of their lives. Many did this.

In this way, we made sure each of them had a chance to become a child of God. So, during those days, we not only prayed for and ministered to Eric, but also to all those who came to see him.

The Word of God came to me during these daily visits with Eric:

> *And we know that in all things God works for the good of those who love him, who have been called according to his purpose.* Romans 8:28

> *Be still and know that I am God;*
>   *I will be exalted among the nations,*
>   *I will be exalted in the earth.*
>   Psalm 46:10

> *Everyone who calls on the name of the Lord will be saved.* Romans 10:13

God is good, no matter what the circumstances of our personal lives may be.

CHAPTER 4

Grown Men Crying

I had never seen so many grown men cry. There were big men, tall men, short men and small men, but they all had one thing in common: they cried when they saw Eric's condition.

Like the rest of us, many of them were in disbelief. How had this happened? And how *could* such a thing happen to a guy as nice as Eric? He never bothered anyone, and everybody loved him. Why would someone—anyone—do this to him?

Some not only cried; they collapsed at times with emotion as they talked about Eric and his good heart. Everyone agreed that he was a very good person.

My answer to this was that what happened to Eric could have happened to any one of them, but it hadn't. I encouraged them to seek God while they had the opportunity.

At the end of each day, as I traveled back home, my mind reviewed everything that had happened that day. I wept and, at one point, I asked God "Why?"

"Why not?" He responded.

It wasn't the answer I wanted or thought I needed to hear in that moment. His Word declares:

> Seek the LORD while he may be found;
>   call on him while he is near.
> Let the wicked forsake their ways
>   and the unrighteous their thoughts.
> Let them turn to the LORD,

and he will have mercy on them,
and to our God,
  for he will freely pardon.

"For my thoughts are not your thoughts,
  neither are your ways my ways,"
    declares the Lord.   Isaiah 55:6-8

At the moment, that didn't seem to make any sense to me. All I could think about was that I wanted my baby healed. I wanted to see God heal him from the crown of his head to the soles of his feet. I wanted him to get out of that hospital bed and run around — go bowling, play basketball, something, anything — to let me know that he was okay. But it wasn't happening.

Day one in that hospital turned into days two, three and four, and then a week had passed. Then week one turned into weeks two, three and four and the beginning of week five. Every single day for those first two weeks, during every single visit, I could hear the Lord saying to me: "Be still and know that I am God! Don't be moved by what you see or hear! I AM IN CONTROL!"

Those words were so real that I repeated them every day, before, during and after every visit. But, although I knew the Lord was with me and in control of the situation with Eric, my heart still ached for him. Seeing him lying there lifeless was so hard for me!

Any mother would have felt the same, in pain to see their son lying there that way and knowing that there was nothing they could do to make him feel better. It was sheer agony.

In Eric's case, I couldn't even do anything to reassure him that he would soon be out of that hospital bed and back home with those who loved him.

It was all so heartbreaking!

Each visit with my son was precious and tear-jerking for me. I would say the promises God had given me. I would pray that God would heal him from the crown of his head to the soles of his feet. I would hold his hand as I talked and sang to him. Then one very special day, Father God allowed me to see His grace and mercy in a new light.

CHAPTER 5

Say the Name

That day I was singing the popular chorus, "Say the Name."

Say the name of Jesus!
Say the name of Jesus!
Say the name so precious!
No other name I know!
Say the name of Jesus!
Say the name of Jesus!
Say the name so precious! [1]

---

1. Words and music by Martha Minizzi, all rights reserved.

While I sang this over and over, I stood by Eric's bed with my right hand on his forehead. Suddenly, tears began to roll down his cheeks, and I lovingly wiped them away. There was such a powerful anointing from God filling the atmosphere of the room that day that it seemed that anything was possible.

Then Eric moved his head and looked my way. As I rushed to wipe away his tears, a new stream of tears begin to roll down my own face. But I kept singing and worshipping the Lord, and not another word was said.

I couldn't help but wonder what was going on in Eric's mind that day. What did he want to say to me? He held and squeezed my hand, but that was as much response as he could muster.

But even though Eric could not talk out loud, I sensed that He was communing with Father God in his spirit, and I gave him a gentle reminder to call on the name of Jesus from his heart, assuring him that God would hear and answer him.

A promise from the Word of God came to me:

Believe in the Lord Jesus, and you will be saved—you and your household.

Acts 16:31

At the age of fourteen, Eric had been saved and started his journey of love with God. He had grown up learning the Word of God and praying. In fact, my husband and I were privileged to be his youth pastors. I was glad to know in that moment that our son's salvation was not in question.

One thing I am sure of and stand on: the promises of God are true. He said:

Start children off on the way they should go,

*and even when they are old they will
not turn from it.* Proverbs 22:6

Eric knew how to pray, he knew the
Word of God, and he had a personal
relationship with God, the God of his
parents, his grandmother and his great-
grandmother.

Every single day, while we were praying and believing for Eric's healing, God
was showing us all His grace and mercy in
operation. "Trust God" was the message
permeating the atmosphere. **Trust God!**

His Word came to mind:

*I will say of the LORD, "He is my ref-
uge and my fortress, my God, in whom
I trust."* Psalm 91:2

It was a sweet reminder of what Father
God had spoken to me that first day as I
was on my way to the hospital:

Say the Name

I am in control!
Don't be moved by what you see or hear!
TRUST ME!

We had no other choice now. God must have a plan for Eric's life. We just had to trust Him.

Chapter 6

Eric's Last Breath

The day Eric took his last breath was a day of excitement for some, but a day of stark reality for me. Doctors had warned us that the end might be near, and we were all gathered around him in the ICU. I remember singing that day the old beloved hymn "I Surrender All."[2] But did I, and could I?

Tears continuously rolled down my face all that day, and I seemed powerless to

2. By Judson W. Van DeVenter 1896, public domain

44

stop them. No sooner had I wiped my face of tears than more tears appeared to take their place. Eventually I stopped wiping them away and concentrated on singing and worshiping God.

Then, suddenly, Eric sat up as if he had just awakened and was ready to go home. He moved his head, his neck and his shoulders, as if to take a big stretch. His dad called the nurse so that she could document the movements.

Until this time, Eric had been breathing with little or no help from the ventilator. Everyone was now watching to see if he would move again.

I held his hand and kept singing and weeping, and Eric moved again. This time, he moved his head, neck and shoulders as before and then did what some later described as taking a big yawn. But I sensed that it was not a yawn. That was my son's last breath.

It soon became apparent that Eric was no longer breathing on his own, as the machines suddenly kicked on and began to breathe for him. I saw the ventilator as it went from him breathing on his own to complete control by the machine itself. I couldn't believe it, but my Eric was making the transition to be with Father God that day. It was day 31, and he had outlived all of the doctors' expectations. But, it seemed, God was intent on taking him home.

Now that Eric's breathing was totally controlled by the ventilator, his lungs were shutting down, his heart rate was decreasing, and he was very quickly all but brain dead. It became obvious that we, his family members, would have to prepare to let him go.

We were *not* faced with the decision of whether or not to discontinue Eric's life support. One by one, all of his vital signs decreased, as each of his organs shut down. He was leaving us.

God knew that we could never have made the decision to pull the plug on our beloved son, so He did it Himself. Just like that, very peacefully, Eric transitioned into the arms of Jesus.

CHAPTER 7

Letting Go

"I surrender all?" Oh, God, how I wanted to do that, but could I? My heart was hurting so badly at that moment.

We tend to ask the whys about everything. And, even when we know what is best, we get selfish and want to keep our loved ones here with us—no matter what. It doesn't matter that the life they once knew will be no more. We still want them here with us. We will take care of them—no matter what. At least, that's what we say, and at that critical moment, we actually believe it. Say what you will, saying goodbye and releasing someone you love to be with the Lord is not an easy matter.

Suddenly we all began to evaluate our individual relationships with Eric.

"Did I do all I wanted to do?"
"Did I say all I needed to say?"

These and many other questions suddenly came to our minds. I was so glad that I had no regrets. Eric and I had openly shared our love and always maintained open lines of communication. He always knew that he could talk to me about anything at all.

Like many young people, he did feel uncomfortable talking to his mother about sex. Every time I would ask questions and try to get him to talk about it, he would answer, "Now, Ma, some things I'm just not 'gonna' talk about, and sex is one of them." I understood.

We'd had so much quality family time, with trips, the family birthday celebrations, the graduations (his and mine), holidays together and so much more. Now it had all come to a startling end, and saying goodbye now seemed so final.

I had to come to grips with the fact that my baby boy, my firstborn, would no longer dwell on earth with our family. With God's help, I purposed in my heart that not only would I celebrate his life; I would celebrate his memory and his transition from earth to Heaven.

In this way, through my tears, brokenhearted and filled with pain, I was able to find peace in God and know that Eric had made a peaceful transition from earth to Heaven. He could now enjoy being with Father God. What could be more wonderful for him?

CHAPTER 8

Saying Our Goodbyes

For the next several days, the house was filled with people coming to express their condolences and to do their best to comfort the family. They meant well, but I just wanted to be left alone.

I didn't want to talk to anyone about how I felt, and I certainly didn't want to know any more about what had happened. All I knew was that my son was gone, never ever to return. I would never hold him again. I could never talk to him again. I could never look into his big brown eyes again. I could never grab his hand and say, "What's new with you, son?" I could never ride in his car and reach to turn the music down or say to him, "Boy, slow this car down!"

So many other "I can'ts" came to my mind, but I forced myself to take a deep breath. Then I took another breath, this one longer and deeper. I had to collect myself, for this was it. The day had come, and I needed to celebrate Eric's life, and yet I was still full of gloom.

Again, so many people were in attendance to celebrate Eric's home-going. I was aware of the fact that some had perhaps come just to see what was going on and how Eric looked, but the majority of the people there had come to support the family and to bid farewell to someone they had loved and were genuinely fond of.

Many of Eric's friends approached us that

day and told us about the fine job my husband and I had done to raise such a great young man. Many talked about his big heart, how kind he was, how friendly he was, how responsible he was.

These were friends of the family, but also people who worked with Eric, socialized with him or went to church with him, and they all spoke highly of him. The elderly among them said that Eric had never met a stranger.

The funeral program that day was inspirational from the beginning to the end. The songs of praise and worship, the prayers, the scriptures read and the sermon all brought comfort, peace and joy to our family.

It did our hearts good to see some young men and women accept the Lord as their Savior during Eric's funeral service. I prayed and continue to pray that each of them would fully pursue a personal relationship with the Lord.

On the Other Side of Through There Is HOPE!

When all of that was eventually over, getting into that funeral-home limousine and riding to the grave-site seemed to be absolutely numbing to my heart, my mind, my body, my soul—to every fiber of my being.

Once again, I just could not believe that I was about to bury my son. My mind just could not fathom the reality of having to let him go and never again have the opportunity to see him here on this earth.

I prayed that somehow the funeral procession would never arrive at the grave-site. Unfortunately, it did, and once there, getting out of the car was so very difficult for me to do. For a moment, I looked out the window and stared at the spot where the coffin was to be laid. I could see that crowds of people had already gathered and were standing there waiting.

Eventually, when I was able to move, I got out of the car, but in slow motion. My legs didn't seem to want to carry me, and the rest of my body was also very slow to respond.

Saying Our Goodbyes

People and flowers were everywhere. Most of the family was able to sit down under the small funeral tent, but some stood nearby for the final parting words of the ceremony.

At that point, I didn't want it to be over, and I didn't want to leave that place. Eventually, my aunt grabbed me by the arm and said, "Dawn, it's time to go!"

I didn't want to go. I didn't want to believe that my son was being laid forever to rest. It was all so surreal!

As I walked away slowly to the car, I was asking myself, "Is this real? Am I really leaving my son here? Was that really his body in that casket? This cannot be real." Unfortunately, it was all too real. I had just buried my firstborn son.

Thank God for the promises of His Word:

We are confident, I say, and would prefer to be away from the body and at home with the Lord.   2 Corinthians 5:8

Very truly I tell you, whoever hears my word and believes him who sent me has eternal life and will not be judged but has crossed over from death to life.

John 5:24

Although I, and my whole family, would have wanted Eric to still be here with us, we knew that he would never have wanted to come back. He was in the best place ever.

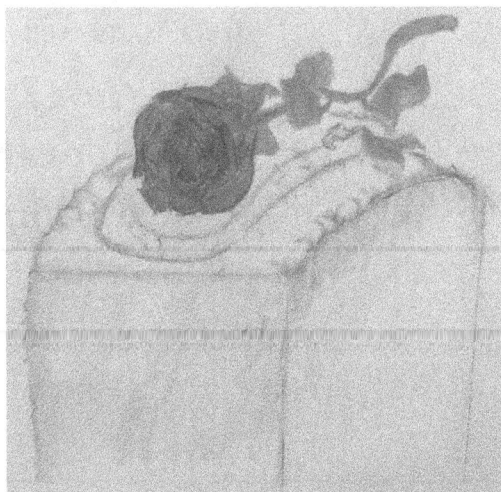

But even with that knowledge, it was so terribly hard to say goodbye!

CHAPTER 9

The Grieving Begins

This next part is the focus of the book and my premise for writing it in the first place. During my own grieving process I could not find a book that comforted me or that I felt brought liberty to my hurting spirit. Therefore it is my desire to be able to share with others the freedom I encountered while walking through this process with God.

Grieving is a process, and I will be the first to admit that the process is not an easy one. It was not an easy one for me. I spent endless days and nights crying and questioning God. Even with the responses I had received from Him previously, I still found myself asking Him *why*? I just couldn't understand it.

Even though my relationship with God had helped me through this entire process, it had been an intensely emotional experience. Even as I sat down to write this book, tears flowed freely from my eyes.

Was there a purpose in it all? Yes, I could feel the cleansing and the healing as each tear fell and rolled down my cheeks. I prayed that as I wrote I would be delivered, restored and made whole, and now I pray that same prayer for you. May you also experience deliverance, restoration and wholeness.

As I began this process, I wasn't sure just what I should be feeling. In many ways, I was a mass of confusion. I seemed unable to put into words what I was going through, and my emotions were all over the place.

From one day to the next, I never knew what to expect. But I did sense that I would have to learn to speak life over myself every day. It was in doing this that I learned to depend upon communion with God in worship and in His Word that I had stored inside my spirit precisely for such a time as this.

During this process, I learned that no two people grieve the same. I had to release my mother from trying to be strong for me, and I had to release myself from trying to be strong for others. We agreed together that it was okay to cry and, at times, we cried together.

Every single day, I would ask myself, "Is this real? Is Eric really gone? Did he really die?" And I had to answer, *"Yes, this is real. He is gone."* I am told that this initial shock and unbelief was a normal part of the grieving process.

There were so many questions running through my mind, and many of them, I knew, might never be answered.

Realizing and acknowledging the fact that my son was gone, that he would never come through the doors of our house again, that I would never have him call me again just to ask, "What are you doing today?" and would never again experience his bear hug was a big step for me. His death was real, and I had to accept it and go on living.

I'm not saying that I have totally accepted his death. As of today, I still can't say that. I just know that he's not here and will never be seen here again. But that doesn't change God and the fact that I am alive and need to go on living, for myself and for others.

CHAPTER 10

Know Who to Tune Out

In this process, I had to learn to tune certain people out. For some strange reason, people will come up to you during your grieving process and say some really crazy things:

Don't cry; be strong!
All is well; just pray and trust God.

I didn't want to hear any of that. I remember thinking that the next person who came up to me and told me to be strong would find out just how strong I could be when I punched their lights out. I was dealing with the loss of my son, and I didn't have any strength at that moment, much less to listen to people who had no idea what I was going through.

They were wrong, dead wrong! There is nothing wrong with crying. Cry if you must. Scream if you must. Write if you must. Whatever you feel you have to do at the time that is helpful to you, so that you can let go of the pain you feel, by all means do it. For me, crying was the beginning of my healing process.

I'm thankful that throughout my entire process, I was able to find comfort in the Lord and in His Word. He reminded me:

For his anger lasts only a moment,
  but his favor lasts a lifetime;
weeping may stay for the night,

but rejoicing comes in the morning.

Psalm 30:5

There were many sleepless nights. It sometimes felt like morning would never come, and I had both good days and bad days. I found comfort and peace only as I buried myself in the Word of God and prayer.

I needed the Lord to keep me sane. I felt like I was at the end of a cliff and actually wanting to jump off. I prayed while I was walking around during the day, and I prayed while I was driving my car. Sometimes I just sat in shock and looked around, wondering what to do next. That, too, was part of the process.

Men and boys sometimes have the perception that crying is not a manly thing to do. When Malcolm confided in me what he was experiencing and told me he didn't think he should cry because he needed to be strong for me, I didn't hesitate to tell him that it was okay for him to cry. "Baby, that was your brother," I said. "It's okay for you to cry, and you do *not* have to be strong for me." We cried together, and with that, the healing began for Malcolm too.

I cannot describe what I felt when I saw tears falling from my husband's eyes. He wasn't too big or too proud to cry. He was hurting too. God had to be there for all of us. We needed one another, and we each had to do what the Scriptures command:

> *Casting all your care upon him; for he careth for you*   1 Peter 5:7, KJV

It was a process that we each had to walk out independently of the others. And you will too. Surrender to the process, and God will be there to help you.

CHAPTER 11

From Tears to Anger

I went from crying to being angry. Was I angry with God? Or was I angry with the people who had caused this terrible thing to happen? Eventually I learned that anger just happened to be another step in the grieving process and the step that I was on at the moment. I didn't understand why I was angry and couldn't even admit that I *was* angry.

Finally I admitted, to myself and to God that I was angry. "Lord," I said, I am angry with You for allowing this to happen, and I am angry at the jerk who hurt my son. How could You have allowed this to happen? And why is it that when I prayed, it seemed to be in vain? Your will has to be done anyway, so why should we even pray?"

For the moment, in my anger, I had forgotten about the words God had given me each day to bring me through this whole ordeal, forgotten how many prayers He *did* answer along the way. Again I was reminded that God was in control of all things.

With my bottled-up emotions, I continued to battle to move forward on a daily basis. There were times when I didn't even want to get out the bed in the morning. I didn't want to do anything. How could I go on living when Eric was gone and would never return?

I felt like a walking zombie, in shock and anger that my son had been stolen from me. It was then that God begin to birth in me the words "On the other side of THROUGH." "Don't you quit," He encouraged, "and don't turn back. You *will* get to the other side." With that in mind, I knew that I needed to trust God and keep moving forward.

CHAPTER 12

Talk Your Way to Your Healing

Talk your way to your healing, refusing to allow guilt to take root and fill your mind with a plague of negative thoughts and emotions. Yes, you will sit at times and wonder, "What could I have said or done differently? Did I say everything I should have said? Did I hang out enough with my loved one? Did we spend enough time doing what he or she loved doing?" But refuse to speak

68

negatively. It leads nowhere. Instead, think and speak positively. Although I thought and rethought through every moment of our life together with Eric, I found, in the end, that I would not have traded a moment of it.

As a family, we made the decision to think on the good times we'd had together, to talk often and to laugh as much as we could when we remembered our times with Eric. In fact, we decided that we would talk at least once a day about something that pertained to him. And we did that. Every day we would remember and laugh (or cry) as we thought back on his life.

We remembered birthday dinners, summer trips, daily, weekly and monthly rituals that he had with any of us. And it was all good.

So TALK, TALK AND TALK some more. It helps. As each day came and went, and we talked and laughed, the pain became a little more bearable, and the days and nights got a little easier.

Realizing that grief is personal and individualized also helps with healing. Allow time for individual grief. We all needed to have time to ourselves, to grieve, and each grieved in his or her own way. I chose to look at our photo albums, to write, to sing and to pray. Others would talk to Eric, read the Bible, play music, throw a kiss toward Heaven and pray to God.

Where I may have been able to look at the photos and smile and laugh through my tears, this was difficult for others. Going into Eric's room and looking at his things was difficult for me at times, but I felt that it was a necessary step for me so that I could continue my process of healing.

Recovery was a journey of ups and downs, for all of us, of good days and bad days, happy days and sad days. The wonderful thing is that God was with us every step of the way.

CHAPTER 13

Be There for Others

Since my purpose in writing this book is to help others who might be going through the same things, I would like to share a little here on *communal* healing. As a friend to someone going through the grieving process, the best thing you can do is to just BE THERE for them. There were times when I just needed someone to talk to, and thank God I had friends like that.

I know that I was sometimes just saying the same things over and over, but it meant a lot to me to have someone willing to listen anyway. I am aware of the fact that this may have made them a little crazy at times, and I am grateful that they didn't give up on me.

We each had our own support groups, those who stood with us and helped us through our grieving processes. Each of them provided words of encouragement, a sense of hope, a shoulder to cry on, listening ears or just an opportunity for us to get away from our own thoughts.

The many people who prayed while Eric was in the hospital now prayed for the Lord of Comfort to be there for us, to strengthen, heal and keep us as we, too, went through a transition of a sort.

During this time, I was very focused on myself and my own hurts, but I later learned (from my extended family) that they, too, were having to deal with Eric's death in their own way. They, too, were hurting and dealing with grief in one of its forms. At the time, many of them did not know what to do or say to help me, for they, too, needed help with their own process. They, too, had loved Eric, who had considered them an aunt or an uncle.

Someone asked me the question: "How can we ever heal from a wound this deep?" It was a question for which I had no real answer at the time. I could think of things to say in response, but my heart and my lips were not yet in agreement. Something more serious was taking place in me now, and I would need another kind of help.

Chapter 14

Get Professional Help!

I began to wonder what was happening to me. I now know that depression was trying to take over my life, my very existence. At times, I seemed to have no fight left within. We can actually become paralyzed by grief, and that was my case.

Sometimes I really didn't want to do anything, and at other times I wanted to do things that I would not normally have done. Some days I just wanted to stay in bed, all curled up into a ball. At other times, I longed to be held and be told: "Everything is going to be fine. You will be okay."

Eventually I had to come to a place of surrender. I needed the help of the Father to make it from moment to moment, from hour to hour and from day to day. I could not exist without His help. I now stood upon His promise:

> *Come unto me, all you who are weary and burdened, and I will give you rest.* Matthew 11:28

I had tried over and over and over again in myself to find rest, but I couldn't. I didn't know how to pray anymore. I didn't know what to say anymore. I was sinking more and more into a quiet shell that I just could not or would not shake. My intense prayer had now become, "Lord, preserve my mind. I need You to keep me sane."

I couldn't understand how I had gone from intense worship of God and fellowship with Him to simply sitting in the church pew, waiting and wondering what would happen next. Once again, I acknowledged that I was angry with God and sought His forgiveness. And He, in His mercy, helped me.

This is a very important chapter. Depression is very real, and anyone suffering from it must seek help. If you feel that you have no way out and can no longer deal with life or the situations life brings your way, by all means, get help!

Too often we have been taught that counseling is not beneficial. "Why do I need counseling?" we sometimes ask. Well, let me tell you that I learned the

hard way that counseling can be extremely helpful. It was for me. If you have a
need, please seek help from a trusted
counselor, preferably one who loves
God and His Word.

Not only had I been feeling depressed; I was also feeling lonely. Yes,
my family and my friends were all
around me and they were available to
me, and yet I still felt so alone. I desperately needed this outside help, and
it set me on a better course.

The counselor helped me to see that
what I was experiencing was common
to all those who grieve, that I was not
abnormal in my reactions, and she
suggested things that helped me get
through each of the stages of grief.

It was this counselor who introduced
me to the idea of writing down my feelings and working through my healing

in that way, so this book is a result of her godly advice. To her, I say, "Thank you," and to God I say, "Thank You for her and other wise people You placed in my life just when I needed them."

CHAPTER 15

Stay Focused on God

One of the most important parts of the healing process is to stay focused on God. If He gives you a word, hold on to that word tightly and refuse to let go of it. Whatever you do, don't allow the enemy to steal that word from you. This is a spiritual battle. God's written Word declares:

> *For though we walk in flesh, we do not war after the flesh; for the weapons of our warfare are not carnal, but mighty through God to the pulling down of*

80

strong holds; casting down imagina-
tions, and every high thing that exalts
itself against the knowledge of God, and
bringing into captivity every thought
to the obedience of Christ; and having
in a readiness to revenge all disobedi-
ence, when your obedience is fulfilled.
2 Corinthians 10:3-6, KJV

I began to look for answers in the Word
to help me recover and come out of this rut
I had allowed myself to become stuck in.
I no longer wanted to feel depressed. I no
longer wanted to be in a state of loneliness.
It was time to get up and move forward,
trusting God's promises.

I cried out to the Lord, "I need You like
never before. I give to You all the anger. I
give to You all the disappointment. I give to
You all the hurt. I give to You all the bitter-
ness. I need You to make me whole again."
He heard that prayer.

CHAPTER 16

Be Willing to Forgive

It was only after I had prayed this prayer that I could begin to pray for the man who had committed this heinous crime against my son. I wasn't at all sure that I really wanted to forgive him, but I asked myself the question:

"How badly do you want to be free?"

And, now, through the pages of this book, I am asking you the same question. Pause now and take some time to think about what has *you* bound. Then think about how badly you want and need to be free. The Word of the Lord comes to mind

Who shall separate us from the love of Christ? shall tribulation, or distress, or persecution, or famine, or naked-ness, or peril, or sword?

Romans 8:35, KJV

The answer to this question is NOTHING! If we make up our minds to it, nothing, absolutely nothing can separate us from the love of God. But we must make up our minds to walk in the liberty He offers.

Freedom is a choice. I came to realize that I could not walk in freedom unless and until I decided to walk in FORGIVENESS.

Forgiving is a very large part of the heal-ing process. I needed to forgive the man who had gone on trial (two years after the fact) and been convicted for the murder of my son. Could I do it? I had no choice. If I wanted to be free, I had to forgive him.

As I struggled through the process, blaming God for not healing Eric the way I wanted Him to and for allowing this person to do such a thing, I was often reminded of the truth of the Scriptures:

God has said,

"Never will I leave you;
never will I forsake you."
Hebrews 13:5

He was with me through it all, and I'm so glad God knows the heart of every man, woman, boy and girl. In my heart, I had been angry. I was hurting. I felt lonely. I felt betrayed. Because of it, depression had tried to consume me. My grief had opened a door to a very real enemy. I had allowed my broken heart to become harder and harder, until it seemed that no one dared to penetrate it. Now I cried out to God:

"Lord, change this stony heart and give me a heart of flesh."

I soon begin to smile and rejoice because right after saying that prayer, I read this promise:

And I will give them one heart, and I will put a new spirit within you; and I will take the stony heart out of their flesh, and will give them an heart of flesh. Ezekiel 11:19 KJV

Thank the Lord He didn't give up on me! So, why should I forgive this man who had done such a terrible thing? So that I could be free! The act of forgiveness was not as much for him as it was for me.

In your case, start by asking yourself, "Who do I need to forgive and for what?" I found that I first needed to forgive myself. We are often thinking, "I could have," "I should have," "I wish I would have ... ." But we didn't, and now we need to forgive ourselves for anything we feel we overlooked or failed in. It's too late now to change it, so we can't do anything about it. We can only live for today and tomorrow. I chose to forgive myself, and it freed me.

Next, I had to forgive God for not letting things turn out the way I had wanted them to. I felt that my son should have lived, and I blamed God that he didn't. I may never understand God's reasons for taking Eric, but then He's God, and I'm not God. He is entitled to His own plans, even when I am not able to understand them. I chose to forgive God, and it freed me some more.

I also had to forgive my son. Why? Because he died. He was supposed to continue to fight. He was supposed to get out of that hospital bed and come home to me. It didn't matter in what state he was in. I just wanted him home. Deep within my heart, I had not wanted to release him to die, but I had to do it. I chose to forgive Eric, and more freedom came.

Then, I had to forgive that guy who caused this whole mess which ended in the death of my son. I so wanted him to die a brutal death and, if looks could kill, every time I went into that courtroom, he would have died. Then, somewhere and at some point, God began to change my heart toward him. I began to cry out to God for mercy for his soul. I cried for God to save him and cause him to see the pain and suffering his decision had caused others. I asked God to help me to walk in total forgiveness and to take away all hate from my heart. I chose to forgive him for Eric's murder, and that brought an ever greater freedom.

I also had to forgive the man's mother. She, too, was responsible for the decision-making process of what led up to her son's actions of violence. She spoke words that encouraged his behavior, and thus, I held her accountable for the death of my son. Forgiving her was one of the hardest things I ever had to do, but I chose to forgive her and that freed me.

CHAPTER 17

Attending the Trial

Attending the trial of the man who had killed my son had been an extremely emotional experience. I sat there with a blank stare on my face, in total shock, as the witnesses were called one by one, and the story of what had happened unfolded.

As this played out, I very much just wanted to get my hands on that guy. If only I could just slap him or punch him or maybe even stab him with a pencil or pen in the head. But, of course, that wouldn't have helped anything, and it wouldn't have brought my son back to me.

Every day the members of the jury studied my face to see how I would react to what was being said. There were two in particular who seemed to be very touched by my pain, a lady and an older gentleman. I could see the reaction in their eyes as the tears rolled down my cheeks unheeded.

Even the judge, it seemed to me, could feel the agony of a mother in pain. I made no audible sounds. Only the tears spoke for me.

Many people had assured me that I would have closure after the trial was over, but I had none. Yes, I was relieved that it was finally over and, yes, I was happy that the jury had found the man guilty on all charges, but no verdict could bring me closure. The closure I wanted was to have my son alive and well, and that wasn't going to happen.

Every day I asked the Lord to help me accept what I could not change. I could not change the facts that my son had died and that he would never be coming home.

I was glad there would be no more visits to that courtroom, so glad that I decided not to attend the sentencing hearing. Emotionally, I was already drained and didn't want to experience any more emotions. I did send the following written words to have read on my behalf to the man whose decision had so drastically changed my life:

I, the Mother Who Miss Her Son

No words can adequately describe the pain I feel on a daily basis because of the loss of my son. I try to

think of all the "what ifs," the "if onlys," but nothing makes sense. I can only find peace in knowing that, as a child, my husband and I made sure he was raised knowing God and having his own relationship with God, so his soul would not perish.

The day of the incident brought shock as I thought, "Why?" Then every day thereafter was more pain, as I stood and watched my son's lifeless body lay and drift away from me day by day.

Releasing him was the hardest decision I have ever had to make in my life. I knew, in that release, I would never get my daily calls just to see what I was doing. I knew I would never get my bear hugs from my little boy, even though he was now a grown man. I knew

I would never hear, "I love you, Mom," ever again from him.

There is a huge hole in my heart that I know, only with the help of God, can be healed. Daily I ask God to keep my mind. Daily I ask God, "Will this pain ever go away?" Daily I ask God, "Will the tears ever stop flowing?"

I've been told in time the pain will go away. I don't think the pain will ever go away. I think, as a people, we just learn to live with it and make adjustments accordingly.

May God help us all!

It was over, and the man who did this unspeakable thing had been sentenced. But I still had no closure, for I had lost my son.

CHAPTER 18

The Ps to Help You Transition from Loss to Gain

Here are some things God showed me that can help those who have suffered loss:

Passion: It's okay to have the feelings that you experience (we all have emotions). It's okay to cry, to be angry, to feel disappointed. The important thing is what to do after that.

The Ps to Help You Transition from Loss to Gain

Preparation: You will have moments when you will just have to press through a tough spot. Pray, pray and pray some more. God will help you!

People: Don't spend too much time alone. You need other people. Spend time with people, talking about your loss and how you feel. Connect with others (new and old), focusing on the people who are here instead of those who have gone on before.

Plan a Distraction: Remember the great times, refusing to focus on the hurt and pain. Learn to shift your focus. What did you enjoy doing with that person? Do it! And, while doing it, laugh and have fun.

Prescription: Write out a plan to do or try something new—forming a foundation in memory of your loved one, performing some community service or volunteering at a church or school. Helping others will help you.

PEACE: Enjoy your quiet times. When you don't feel like being with anyone else, it's okay. Pamper yourself. Have a day out with yourself. Enjoy a movie, a lunch or a dinner alone.

Most importantly:

PRAY, PRAY, AND PRAY some more!

CHAPTER 19

In Closing

Friend, in closing, I encourage you to find peace within yourself. Do whatever you have to do. What do you think will bring you peace and benefit you in the long run? Do it. Below are a few suggestions to help you get started.

- Journal your thoughts
- Exercise
- Sing
- Draw
- Dance

- Travel
- Motivate others
- Walk the dog
- Write poems, songs, books, etc.
- Take photographs of nature
- Take a long hike in the mountains
- Enjoy listening to the waves at the beach.
- Do whatever brings you peace!

Now say this simple prayer with me:

Father God,

I thank You for Your Spirit, which comforts me as I go through this time of transition. I will look to You, for I know my help comes from You. I will trust You, Lord, with my whole heart, as You guide me through my process. Thank You for making me whole.

In Jesus' name,
Amen!

In Closing

Although this book was inspired by the death of my son, I pray that you were blessed, healed, delivered and now have **HOPE**. And remember, in life, we go through various processes, but know that *On the Other Side of "Through," There Is Hope*!

It's Not Time To Die, Young People!

The lives of the children are in limbo.
The hearts of the same are waxing
cold.
In a world of complacency,
The answer's not in you or me.

For we must turn from our own way.
Through God and His mercy,
His love everlasting,
The truth is His Word,
His voice can be heard.

Cry out for the young man who can
be changed,
For it's not their time to die.

Know that salvation is for all.
So is life, until you're called.
Don't let them slip into the pit to fall.
Let them know God is in control.

He can give peace to their troubled souls.
It's not their time to die.

Who will stand for them to fight,
Let them know the ways that are right?
Who will show them the way of God's love,
The kind you get only from above?
Who will let them know that it's not time to die?

Life is given to all.
Choose to live!
Choose to give!
Choose to love!

IT'S NOT TIME TO DIE, YOUNG PEOPLE!

Take a few notes as you reflect on your loss.

_____

_____

_____

_____

_____

_____

_____

_____

_____

_____

_____

_____

_____

_____

_____

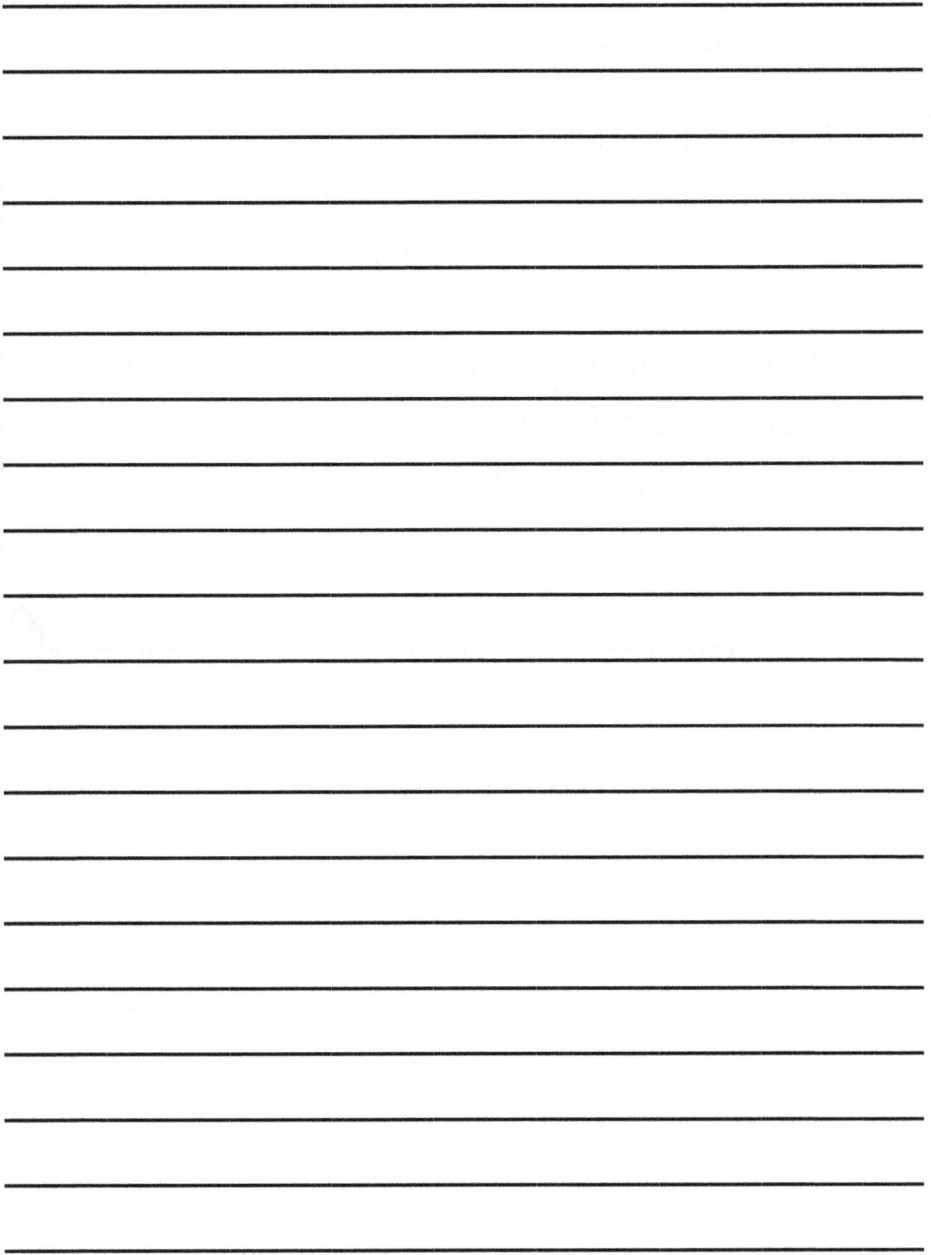

He that dwelleth in the secret place of the most High shall abide under the shadow of the Almighty. I will say of the LORD, He is my refuge and my fortress: my God; in him will I trust.

Psalm 91:1-2, KJV

About the Author

Dawn Greay, aside from being an educator by profession, is also a prophetic psalmist by ministry.

In the field of education, she is currently a Reading Specialist, but her professional experience includes: Educational Consultant, Assistant Principal, 9th Grade Academy Principal, Marketing Coordinator, Finance Academy Director, School To Career Coordinator, High Schools That Work Coordinator and Business/Math Teacher.

She is the owner of E&M Designs and Destiny Learning Academy.

She has an M.A. +30 in Curriculum and Instruction/Reading Specialist Degree, an M.A. in Administration and Educational

Leadership and a B. S. in Secondary Business Education.

She has the following certifications:

- Reading Specialist
- Secondary School Principal Grades 6-12
- Principal Grades K-12
- Marketing Education
- Business Education
- Business and Office Education.
- The IC3 Certification (Internet and Computer Core Certification).

Dawn has been an ordained minister since 2001 and has served in the following capacities in ministry:

- Youth Pastor
- Minister of Music (Prophetic Psalmist)
- Elder
- Board member – Finance Executive

She is a member of the following social and professional organizations:

- Alpha Kappa Alpha Sorority Incorporated since 1991
- MEA (Marketing Education Association)
- ASCD (Association for Supervision and Curriculum Development)
- Phi Theta Kappa Honor Society
- Kappa Delta Phi International Honor Society in Education
- The Board of New Millennium College Tours

Author Contact Page

You may contact Dawn Greay for speaking engagements in the following ways:

eMail: dawnbg71@gmail.com

or

Telephone: 504.919.4366

* 9 7 8 1 9 4 0 4 6 1 9 3 9 *